Land of Strangers:
A visitor's guide to Danag'ombe, Naletale, Zinjanja and Bhila Heritage Sites, Insiza District, Zimbabwe

Paul Hubbard

Pigeon Press

Published by Pigeon Press

For more information on this and other titles, please email:
info@hubbardstours.com

ISBN: 978-1-77929-330-5
ISBN (eBook): 978-1-77921-157-6

Publication © 2021

First Edition

Acknowledgements
I am grateful to Violette Kee-Tui, Jono Waters, Lesley Machiridza, Phephile
Tshabangu, Rita Normanton and Bill Dally for their assistance while writing
this booklet. Tammy Honiball kindly redrew the maps, combining various
sources. I remain responsible for any errors and all interpretations offered.

Also available from Pigeon Press
A Short History of Bulawayo 1868-2017 — by Paul Hubbard
The Boy Who Loved Camping — by John Eppel
Mulberry Dreams — by Violette Kee-Tui

Forthcoming titles from Pigeon Press
Umvukela! The year 1896 in Matabeleland — by Paul Hubbard
A Dream of Souls: The Rock Art of the Matobo Hills — by Paul Hubbard
Bulawayo Blended: an architectural and social history of an African city —
by Paul Hubbard
Not The Whispering Wild — by John Eppel
A Colonial Boy — by John Eppel
Parliament of Animals and Who's Wise — by Lewis Ndlovu

Introduction

This guide focuses on just four of the more spectacular and interesting of the stone-built ruins found in the Midlands province in Zimbabwe. Collectively, these and several others in the area, formed a network of towns ruled first by the Torwa and then the Rozvi peoples from the late 16th to 19th centuries, when they were conquered by the Ndebele people during the *mfecane* upheavals, caused by the violent founding of the Zulu kingdom.

The cluster of ruins in the Midlands area of Zimbabwe is the densest known in the region and, at the time of writing, is deservedly on the Tentative List for inclusion on the UNESCO World Heritage List. There are more than 50 well-preserved ruins packed into an area of 314Km², most with spectacular wall decoration. Importantly for future research projects, most sites were left relatively undisturbed by depredations of treasure hunters and amateur archaeologists who did so much damage to related sites across the country in the 1890s.

The four drystone walled sites chosen for inclusion in this brief guide are representative of the culture as a whole. They have custodians on duty who, in addition to gladly showing visitors around, are there to protect the sites and work towards their long-term conservation.

Location of sites mentioned in the text

I hope you will enjoy visiting these sites as I have many times, in the company of guests, friends and family, revelling in the magnificent achievements of these immensely talented peoples and imagining a wondrous era long before any of us lived.

The Natural World

Located between the cities of Gweru and Bulawayo, it is easy to pass through the Insiza district on the main road without realising the wealth of the natural world surrounding you.

Granite dominates the geology of the area, formed deep within the earth's crust between 2.6 to 2.8 billion years ago. Long periods of erosion and weathering have exposed the granite, leaving behind precariously balanced piles of rocks interspersed with large smooth-sided hills, known locally as *dwalas*. Porous sandy soils are derived from the granites, which suit traditional cereal crops such as millet and sorghum and encourage the growth of the extensive grasslands in the region, so important for the cattle industry, past and present.

There is a small Greenstone Belt in the area, formed an estimated 2.7 billion years ago, an important source of gold, even today. Greenstone is a collection of metamorphic rocks, so named because of the typical greenish hue from various trace minerals. Containing basalt, these rocks often give rise to fertile soils, reddish in colour, and are able to host a wide variety of crops. The various clays derived from this area were crucial for making pottery and plastering hut walls and still are today.

General view of the landscape in the Fort Rixon/Shangani area

Generally speaking, the region is quite dry, with annual rainfall ranging between 450-650mm a year, mostly falling in summer. In recent years, climate change has seen flash storms pounding the area, causing severe flooding. Periodic droughts and long dry spells have become the norm. These inhibit agriculture and encourage people to either start gold mining, which creates massive environmental damage, or to leave the region. During winter, bitingly cold winds and misty conditions are common, notably across the Somabula Flats.

There are several rivers in the area, the major one, the Shangani rising here, and becoming a large river, joining with the Gwayi to flow into the Zambezi. During wetter times in the past, there were several perennial springs which would have supplied humans and animals with water for the entire year.

The vegetation of the area is fairly varied, with forests dominated by *Senna singueana* and *Colophospemum mopane*. Other common woody species include *Combretum*, *Euphorbia*, *Sclerocarya*, *Ziziphus*, *Brachystegia*, *Terminalia*, *Vachellia* and *Albizia*. Interspersed with the forests which hug the hills, are rolling grasslands made up of several species meeting a number of needs from thatching to grazing.

This is one of the finest cattle countries in the region, thanks to the favourable combination of climate, terrain and vegetation. The industry has existed here for at least 2,000 years, and it is thought that control of cattle was as important an economic resource as gold mining and growing crops to the people living here in times past.

Herringbone (top) & Check Decoration

A Long Human History

The prehistory of the Midlands District is rather poorly known compared to other areas of Zimbabwe, so only a general overview is offered.

Early Stone Age (ESA) tools over a million years old are commonly discovered along the river banks. A major site once existed on Gweru Kopje, a factory site where hundreds of tools were made at least 130,000 years ago. This site has since been destroyed by building activities as the city has expanded. Acheulean handaxes, teardrop-shaped ESA tools, were used for everything from cutting meat to stripping bark from branches. Other tools included cleavers, heavy-duty cutting implements suitable for dismembering a carcass and breaking bones to get at the nutritious and delicious marrow within. For more than a million years, these elegantly made creations helped our ancestors to survive and thrive in the region.

Acheulean Handaxe

The Middle Stone Age (MSA) started approximately 250,000 years ago and ended around 40,000 years ago. In Zimbabwe, little is known about this era beyond the variations in the size and shape of the stone tools and scattered hints at the exciting changes in human cognitive makeup on our way to becoming modern human beings. It is during this period of time that the first jewellery, rock art and art mobilier appeared, hafting technology was invented and bone was first used as a raw material for tools. Such revolutions in technology and thought are not that surprising when one considers that our own species, Homo sapiens, emerges in southern Africa within this same time period and migrates to the rest of the world.

The Late Stone Age (LSA), dating from 13,000 to 1,500 years ago, is perhaps the best known time period in the Stone Age of Zimbabwe, simply because it has been the focus of most research efforts. In general, stone tools became much smaller, rarely larger than 2cm; such miniature tools are known as microliths. By creatively combining flakes of stone, fragments of bone and pieces of wood, they were able to create tools for digging, cutting, carving, hunting, sewing, drilling and more.

There are several rock art sites in the region, but most are poorly known and none are currently open to the public, except one small site at Danag'ombe. It is now accepted by most researchers that the art is an integral part of the complex religion of the ancient hunter-gatherers, containing layers of meaning and significance. The art was a crucial part of multi-faceted religious ceremonies which included dancing, singing, medicines, prayers to God and ancestral spirits and perhaps other beings from beyond the veil of the real world. Humans, animals and the other subjects in the art were symbols and metaphors, neatly encapsulating complex spiritual beliefs in the same way that a crucifix does for a Christian in the modern world.

From around 2,400 years ago, a large, sustained migration of people, known to archaeologists and linguists as the Bantu, had begun in West Africa, bringing with it a whole new way of life. These new people travelled in small groups over a distance of almost 3,000 kilometres for a period of two centuries, each generation moving into hospitable new lands, propelled and sustained by forces unknown. Technology changed rapidly, iron and copper replacing stone as the preferred raw material for tools and weapons. Food sources were broadened to include a range of domesticated crops and animals such as cattle, sheep, sorghum, millet and cowpeas, usually complemented by wild fruits and animals.

With time, social complexity grew, propelled initially by internal factors including trade in food, salt, metals and domestic animals. From AD 900, we see the development of international trade to the south in the Shashi-Limpopo confluence area. There, elephant ivory, animal skins, copper and, much later, gold, built on these trends and encouraged the development of a series of states known collectively as the Zimbabwe Culture. Rather than a sharp break, what took place was a gradual cultural change starting over a millennium ago.

Some of the earliest centralised states were Schroda, Bambandanyalo (or K2), Mapela and Mapungubwe, the last now a World Heritage Site. Flourishing from AD 1000 to 1300, the area along the Limpopo saw the emergence of key institutions of later states, including kingship, craft specialisation, urban life and centralised control over many resources. Mapungubwe became the dominant political and commercial centre, controlling a vast trade network and an agriculturally-based economy.

When Mapungubwe's reign ended, thanks to an unwholesome cocktail of declining and erratic environmental, political and external factors, Great Zimbabwe, which had emerged by AD 1250, rose to prominence. It flourished from AD 1300 to 1550, leaving behind some of the most spectacular stone walls in existence. Its leaders were powerful owing to their unchallenged grip on local and international trade, coupled with its crucial position in the politics, economy and religion of populations in central southern Africa. Great Zimbabwe remains one of the most studied sites in the world, largely owing the misguided and unnecessary controversy over its origins. It is a completely indigenous development. For sheer size, Great Zimbabwe is where stone walling reached its grandeur as symbols of the wealth and power of the elites living here.

View over the Hill Complex at Great Zimbabwe

Following a combination of political squabbles, environmental changes and the rise of rivals, Great Zimbabwe faded into obscurity, to be overtaken by two main successor states. Recent research indicates that neither of these states was a direct offshoot of Great Zimbabwe, but, instead, rose up in the vacuum left by Great Zimbabwe's decline. In the north was the Mutapa State, eventually centred along the Zambezi River, famous for its interactions with the Portuguese from the 16th to 18th centuries.

To the west was the Khami State, now thought to have been a semi-independent polity named Butua by the time of Great Zimbabwe's decline, and founded by the Torwa people. They ruled a very successful state, which flourished from AD 1450 to the 1680s, with influence stretching from the Kalahari to the west and south towards the Soutpansberg Mountains in northern South Africa. Buildings of the Khami State were lavishly decorated, as was their beautiful pottery and jewellery. Their cattle wealth and dominance in local trade in food, salt and metals, along with a near-monopoly of the external trade network in southern Zimbabwe, made them a target.

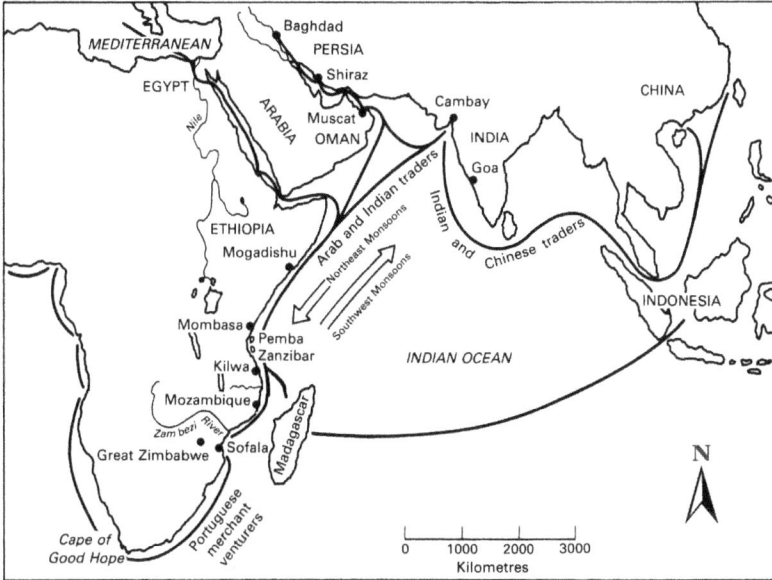

Map showing the Indian Ocean trade network over different eras.
(Modified from K. Shillington. 2012. *History of Africa. 3rd edition.* London: Macmillan)

Probably originating in the Mutoko area, the Rozvi people, a powerful and militaristic group under the command of the Chamgamire dynasty, invaded Butua in about 1683 and overthrew the Torwa leaders. They kept the material culture, political organisation and structures of the previous rulers intact, merely replacing the leadership. Archaeologist, Lesley Machiridza, has spent 15 years unravelling the differences between the Torwa and Rozvi in the archaeological record. Subtle divergences in weapons, pottery styles, trade goods and house construction have been observed by him.

Recent research has suggested that Khami was not a direct successor to Great Zimbabwe, but was, rather, an independent entity which made the most of its environmental and economic advantages to gain great growth and power. It is likely that this kingdom was riven by competition, leading to sustained power-grab attempts, manifested in the archaeological record in new and diverse settlements, exemplified by those forming the subject of this booklet. This era was also epitomised by architectural innovations as aspiring candidates to the throne sought to outdo each other. With the Rozvi takeover in the early 1680s, they maintained Torwa building traditions and inscribed new identities on inherited cultural features. From the 1600s to the 1800s, it would appear that Danag'ombe, Naletale, Zinjanja and Manyanga alternated as centres of political power. There was no clear linear sequence of succession.

In the 1830s the impact of the *mfecane* was felt on the Zimbabwean plateau. Various Nguni groups fleeing Shaka's Zulu kingdom bludgeoned their way through the local population, dismantling the political structures in the process. The first invader was a Swazi Queen, Nyamazana, who besieged Danag'ombe, allegedly forcing the last Rozvi king, Chirisamhuru, to take refuge at Manyanga in the north. She later married King Mzilikazi. The Ngoni, under Zwangendaba, attacked Manyanga, and Chirisamhuru was either killed or committed suicide. The Ndebele arrived in 1838, conquering the entire area, building their own villages and towns throughout the Midlands. With the advent of this new society, language and customs, the art of stonewalling was lost, and many of the old settlements were abandoned, or became sacred sites, only visited by a privileged few.

European hunters, explorers, missionaries and traders soon made their way into the area. As the colonial frontier shifted forward, Cecil Rhodes and his British South Africa Company, by fair means and foul, colonised the country, starting in 1890. A short but bloody war was fought with the Ndebele in 1893, toppling King Lobengula and adding Matabeleland to other British possessions in Africa. A war of resistance was fought by the Ndebele in 1896, known locally as the *Umvukela*, which ended in peace negotiations between them and the white settlers. Thus the Midlands area was opened up for exploration, which is when many of the ruins were revealed to the outside world.

Gweru was originally an Ndebele settlement named *iKwelo* — steep place — after the river's high banks. The modern town was founded in 1894, as a military outpost. It later developed as an agricultural centre and was linked to the railway in 1902. It became a municipality in 1914. Today it is the centre of Zimbabwe's air force training school home to several minor industries and serves as the local agricultural supply centre. It is home to the Military Museum, and a pleasant morning may be had walking the streets admiring several fine historic buildings in the city centre.

Gweru city centre, 1940s

Fort Rixon (National Monument No. 85) was established at the end of August 1896, as a military outpost during the *Umvukela*; built of stone, the fort survives to this day. There is a small cemetery below the hill for those killed during the war in the area. Today a small police outpost watches over this agricultural area, home to several ranching and tree-nut plantation projects. From 1895, much of the area had been subdivided into white-only commercial farms, most taken over under the Zimbabwean government's chaotic and controversial land acquisition exercise, beginning in the year 2000. Scattered villages and fields now form the majority of the landholdings.

A significant new development in the Insiza area is the Shangani Sanctuary, established in the late 2010s. This 89,000ha area is fenced to provide space for eco-tourism and agricultural initiatives. The vision is to allow for the outsourcing of crops and cattle productivity, allowing the inhabitant families to become financially viable and to encourage them to become reliant on the preservation of all wild flora and fauna species. This will hopefully create a lasting and stable ecosystem, encompassing sound agricultural practices.

Notes on Stone Ruins of the Zimbabwe Culture

There are hundreds of stone-built ruins across the Zimbabwe Plateau. Their distribution stretches into parts of Botswana, South Africa and Mozambique. These were the homes of the elite ruling the pre-colonial Shona states. Most date to between AD 1300 and 1830. Few have been adequately investigated by professional researchers but as large-scale research programmes, often sponsored from abroad, gather pace, we will continue to learn more about these settlements and the fascinating culture which produced them.

For over a century there have been often racist and deeply misguided attempts to link the ruins to foreign influences, ranging from the Phoenicians to the Lost Tribes of Israel. There is no doubt that the ruins were the product of an independently-developed, indigenous African culture which had connections to the outside world. Much time and effort has been wasted debating fringe ideas, whose erroneous conclusions have distracted research focus away from more productive avenues.

The stonewalls are only part of a much bigger site and were usually the centre of a town or city. Most people lived in thatched houses, built with clay (*daga* or *dhaka*) plastered onto a wooden frame. Even the elite lived in such houses within the stonewalls, although theirs were much larger, made of thick, multiple layers of compacted dhaka forming what looks like cement.

The stone walls were prestige symbols built to flaunt the owners' wealth and power over others. Their primary purpose was not defensive but did give an element of security and privacy to the elites.

No cement was used in wall construction as each block is placed on another, the best of which form even courses, some punctuated with decoration. Some walls were plastered with clay, which was often coloured with pigments and polished to a high sheen, as a form of decoration.

The stone blocks were quarried from granite. Fire heated the rock, which was cooled by drenching the surface with water which accelerated natural exfoliation. Using iron chisels and cobble hammers, stone masons would shape the blocks to create a neat outer skin, while chunks of rock were used behind these façades as fill. Dolerite, ironstone and quartz were used for decoration in the wall.

Almost all of the ruins in this booklet, as well as many others in the region, have various forms of decoration built into the walls. Archaeologist, Tom Huffman, whose ideas on the interpretation of the use of space and symbolism at Zimbabwe Culture sites are the most influential, suggests the wall patterning is a complicated symbolic code. For example: cord = water snake for female fertility; chevron = fertility of the earth or young men; check = male crocodile for an older man of senior, royal status; herringbone = female crocodile for an older woman of senior, royal status; banded = spirit world and water. The monoliths potentially symbolise the "horns of the mambo", signifying the ability and duty of the ruler to protect his people and lands. Huffman's ideas are controversial and should not be taken as fact; they are based on one interpretation of history and ethnography and are the subject of considerable debate among researchers.

All of the sites show signs of change, growing and shrinking over time. They show little sign of being completely pre-planned, and were changed to suit the needs and whims of the rulers and populace.

It is likely that the sites were arranged in a loose hierarchy with large capitals surrounded by smaller provincial capitals and local administrative centres, some with specialised functions. Others were likely allied to more powerful centres of control. Across the land were also located smaller villages, which focused on agriculture and mining, as well as religious sites.

There is a great deal of healthy academic debate over the interpretation of the history of these settlements, their relationship to one another and the symbolic or other meanings of each site. Multiple sources of evidence, including archaeology, history, ethnography and anthropology are used to create a narrative for each site, although what is presented in this booklet remains a likely scenario. As more research is done, the story will certainly alter to incorporate new evidence and theory; such is the way of the science and practice of archaeology.

Cord Decoration

Danag'ombe Heritage Site

Danag'ombe, the second capital of the Torwa kingdom, was built and occupied between the early 15th and late 19th centuries. It is smaller than Khami, although it shares many of the same architectural and symbolic features. In fact, Khami may have looked just like this at one stage in its development. It is the third largest ruin in the region and visitors should plan at least half a day to fully explore the many fascinating features of this ancient town.

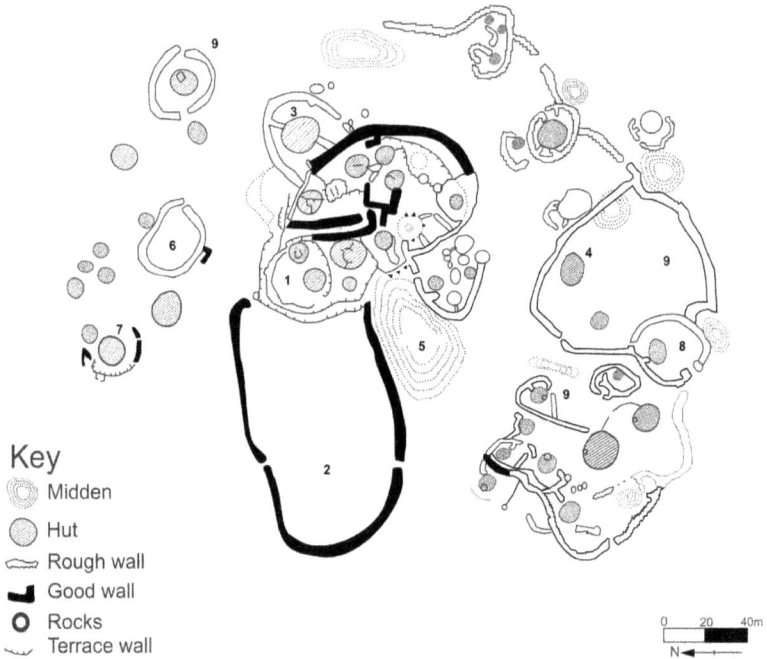

Key

◎ Midden
● Hut
〰 Rough wall
◢ Good wall
O Rocks
〰 Terrace wall

0   20   40m

N

Map of Danag'ombe

Throughout history, the site has variously been called Mambo, Danag'ombe, Danan'ombe and Dhlo Dhlo, the last, named for an Ndebele induna who lived in the area at the time of colonisation and not, as some have suggested, for the head ring once worn by chiefs. An early Ndebele name for the ruins was *amaTangala kaMambo* — stone walls of the *mambo* (king). Another early name on record is Matangoni, an old Kalanga name meaning "the graves". The preferred name today is Danag'ombe, *Ng'ombe* meaning "cattle" and *danga* meaning "cattle byre" in the modern Kalanga language. It is National Monument No. 5, declared on 16 July 1937.

The Torwa, as oral accounts relate, were the first rulers to build and then occupy this site. They were conquered by the Rozvi people who migrated from the north-east and made Danag'ombe their capital from the 1690s until the 1830s.

Danag'ombe covers 1.2 km², comprising about 700ha of settlement debris, although the main platforms occupy just 1.21ha of the entire site. The site, especially the area around the main platform, has been excavated numerous times. The first to excavate it were treasure seekers in the 1890s, followed by Franklin White in 1900, David Randall-MacIver in 1905, Gertrude Caton-Thompson in 1929, Roger Summers in 1959 and National Museums and Monuments of Zimbabwe officials and students in the 1970s, 1990s, 2005 and, lastly, by a multidisciplinary team of various university researchers in 2016. Despite all of this investigation, the chronology and history of the site remains poorly understood, in part because of damage by treasure hunters which hindered subsequent investigations and, equally damaging, the lack of publication of analyses by successive generations of archaeologists.

This ruin is famous as the site of a massive discovery of gold by treasure hunters. The first was Hans Sauer in early 1894, followed by Frederick Burnham, an adventurous American mercenary who had fought in the Anglo-Ndebele War of 1893. He found 20kg (641 ounces) of gold in late 1894. In May 1895, W.G. Neal and George Johnson dug up five graves containing gold jewellery weighing nearly 6.5kg. They further discovered a cache of 21kg (700 ounces) of gold made of nuggets, foil and flakes on the Main Platform. These destructive diggings and spectacular finds led to the formation of the Ancient Ruins Mining Company Limited, which for five years did untold damage to scores of ruins countrywide as the employees and shareholders greedily enriched themselves at the expense of our heritage. Cecil Rhodes acquired some of these finds, which are on display at Groote Schuur, his old home in Cape Town. The rest have disappeared.

The Main Platform (1), focus of the central royal area, was built atop a low granite outcrop which was extended by building retaining walls and backfilling them, forming several terraces along the way. Excavations in 1929, showed that there were at least two episodes of platform building. The first platform, damaged by treasure hunters in the 1890s, was restored in the mid-2000s. It is hidden behind the three decorated tiers visible today. The decoration includes check, chevron, banded and cord designs.

Extending out from the front of the Main Platform is a low-walled oval enclosure (2) that was once decorated in sections with banded, check and cord patterns at intervals. Today much of this wall has fallen down, mostly owing to damage from stray cattle and careless visitors clambering over it. This enclosure was probably the dare, a court where issues of national importance were discussed, decisions made and noteworthy cases tried. It may have also served as a parade ground for Rozvi soldiers, once they had taken over. At one time the enclosure was also used to corral cattle, shown by the ancient deposits of dung at its western end.

Close up of the walling on the Main Platform

The main entrance to the platform is on the northern side and is now entered through a modern breach in the wall. The original doorway was probably a little further along to the north-east. On reaching the top a sunken passageway can be seen; its entrance was probably roofed with wooden poles to hold up a low stone wall across the top. Today, this passageway is closed with a wall, forcing visitors to the left and into one of several internal enclosures.

A lower enclosure in this area has floors from several large dhaka houses, perhaps once occupied by some of the senior royal wives. When excavated in 1929, several burials were located in this area. One grave housed two women buried on the floor of a hut which had been burnt down. The women had died and been buried before the hut was burnt and may have been wives of the king. Their bodies were richly adorned with gold beads and iron and bronze bangles, in addition to imported and local cloth. One of the women wore nearly 0.5kg of bronze wire and bracelets on each arm and nearly 2kg of the same on her legs, indicating her senior status in life.

The western side of the Main Platform, being higher, contains several floors of large huts that once stood here. These were probably for the exclusive use of the ruler and included huts for religious purposes, eating and sleeping. The ruler may have exclusively occupied the two large huts at the apex of the platform, from which he would have been able to survey all in his power. It may have been here that the gold miners recovered a highly decorated soapstone monolith, now in the site museum. It may represent the authority and power of the kingship. Lower down to the south is the massive hole dug by Burnham and others in their quest for treasure. The ruler's senior wife may have lived on this lower tier, where grain bin foundations and lower grindstones were once discovered.

Attached to the back of the main platform is the Kitchen Enclosure (3), where catering was done for the resident royals. There are steps down into it, from the platform above, for the service team. The servants carried ingredients, wood and water and removed waste, entering through a door on the south-western side. There is a large midden (rubbish heap) just beyond this entrance full of ash and kitchen scraps.

Soapstone monolith

To the south-west, still on the Main Platform, are the remnants of a huge grain bin (4). It probably held whole grain sent as tribute to the ruler and would have been under the control of his senior wife. Grain from here would have been distributed to the poor and infirm — people like widows, albinos and those with a disability. The king's wives would possibly have taken threshed grain from an adjacent small grain bin to brew beer, itself a form of currency and an essential part of many rituals and ceremonies.

Next to this grain bin is a rocky outcrop. The gaps between boulders have been closed off with stone walling to the same height, creating a private space. Beneath the boulder on the furthest end and, among the lichen, see if you can spot the rock art: small, red human figures and remnants of antelope, which predate the walling by several centuries. The rock art was created by hunter-gatherers as part of their religious and spiritual rituals, and several authors have theorised that the later Torwa and Rozvi inhabitants took inspiration from this and conducted important rituals and ceremonies here too. Presumably the space would have been used by the king and senior spirit medium resident at the site. This rock art is perhaps the clearest indication that the site was occupied in Stone Age times; MSA and LSA tools and flakes are often seen on the paths and platforms around the site.

K'ang Hsi porcelain found at Danag'ombe

Between this area and the dare is the massive court midden (5). This rubbish heap contains ash, potsherds, bones and other debris from the palace area, accumulated in one spot to avoid the possibility of witchcraft malpractice. The rubbish heap would have grown constantly, people adding ash from fires, bones of animals slaughtered at feasts, broken beer pots, discarded tools and artefacts and more. Such a large midden indicates a very active court. Excavations in 1905, revealed that a layer of clay was placed on the surface of the growing midden at irregular intervals, presumably to keep the dust down during windy weather.

Many interesting finds were discovered in the court midden. These include spears of different sizes, worked ivory fragments, soapstone pipe bowls, copper and iron bangles, ivory, glass, porcelain and shell beads, fragments of K'ang Hsi porcelain, copious amounts of decorated pottery, spindle whorls and broken glass gin bottles, indicating external trade lasted well into the 18th Century.

This is where two pairs of slave shackles (handcuffs and leg irons) were discovered in 1905, with a third pair (handcuffs) discovered near the main platform in 1967. They likely date to the end of the 16th century. One pair of handcuffs shows evidence of having been made locally, with punched instead of forged holes on the shackles. The leg irons show signs of local repair, one cuff being much lighter than the other which may have been a replacement. There is little evidence for slave trading south of the Zambezi River before the 19th century, although the Portuguese would take and sell people into slavery if the opportunity presented itself. Exactly how these artefacts came to Danag'ombe is impossible to deduce with certainty but they may have been used to restrain Portuguese prisoners, captured during the Rozvi raids on the trading post of Dambarare in the 1690s.

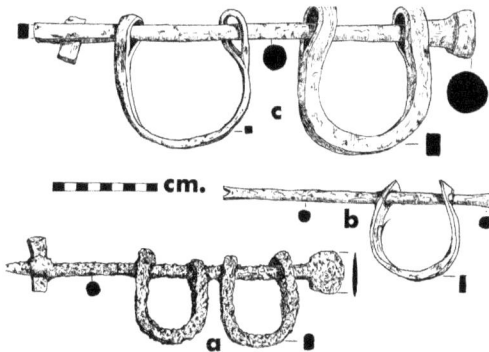

Slave shackles found at Danag'ombe. (a) & (b) handcuff (c) leg irons. (From Cooke 1988).

To the north of the Main Platform is a roughly-built circular enclosure (6) which served as an animal pen. It probably housed a small herd of cattle, providing meat and milk for the personal use of the ruler. Most of the kingdom's cattle were scattered among several cattle posts throughout the country. A small protruding square wall on one side was probably closed off with wooden posts to form an enclosure for young animals. These were traditionally kept separated in such pens to avoid harm coming to them from adult animals. There is a hut mound next to this enclosure which was probably the residence of the herders.

The Northern Platform (7), sometimes erroneously referred to as the Cannon Platform, is a large decorated platform whose wall peters out to merge with the granite dwala on which it is built. It is surrounded to the east by numerous grain bin remains. It was the residence of a senior person at court, but who, precisely, remains enigmatic. It was between this platform and the Main Platform that two Portuguese cannon were discovered lying abandoned on the ground by Hans Sauer on his visit in May 1894. He removed

One of the cannon found at Danang'ombe, in an historical picture from Groote Schuur

them and gave them to Cecil Rhodes. They are currently on display at Groote Schuur in Cape Town. One of the cannons is marked with the Portuguese Coat of Arms. The presence of these cannons, in the opinion of some researchers, marks this as Changamire Mambo's capital, as he would have been the only person allowed to keep such weapons.

In an arc around the Main Platform are several enclosures and low platforms. There has been limited archaeological work in these areas and ideas as to their purpose is speculative.

One of the more interesting is the large enclosure immediately to the south of the Main Platform, containing a low stone platform (8) surrounded by at least 22 grain bin foundations, hut foundations and lines of stones that may have held a wooden palisade. One particularly large structure has two or more doors, and a small, raised clay-built dais. These features hint that this building possibly served as a *banya*. This was a ceremonial building reserved for ritual activities, most crucially *bira*, or spirit possession ceremonies. It was a place for the extended family to gather to offer sacrifice, give thanks and communicate with the ancestors through a spirit medium, known as a *svikiro*. There were larger and more complex *mabanya* for the use of the whole community, where issues such as land claims, food security and conflict resolution were brought to the fore and openly discussed until they were amicably settled, using advice from the ancestors transmitted via the *svikiro*.

In an arc to the south of the dare are a number of small, interlocking enclosures (9). There are house remains within each enclosure, inside which would have lived several members of the elite. We are not sure exactly whom, although some authors have suggested the many junior wives of the ruler may have made their homes here. It is also possible that these and other enclosures at the site were built and occupied by elite members of society at irregular times. It cannot be assumed that the entire site was fully occupied at the same time. Like in any town, some areas would have been abandoned temporarily before finding new purpose as needs changed.

There are a number of foreign finds at Danag'ombe, showcasing its integration into the rich global trade networks that existed during the lifetime of the site. Most of the

Globular pots and gin bottle discovered during excavations in 1929.

Chinese stoneware found at the site is from the K'ang Hsi period, dating from the late 17th to mid-18th centuries. The similarity of these and other trade goods discovered at Danag'ombe, hints at a possible trading connection to the Portuguese *feira* (trading post) of Dambarare, located just to the north of present-day Harare, and which traded in similar items. They may have also been loot from the Rozvi raids.

The Sacred Heart gold medallion
(From Garlake 1973)

Early treasure hunters found several artefacts associated with Catholic priests. A gold medallion with two pelicans and the Sacred Heart may have belonged to a Jesuit priest, likely dating after 1725. This was given to Leander Jameson. A Jesuit priest's signet ring issued by Evora Missionary College in Portugal was also found. Several of the Jesuit missionaries who came to southern Africa from 1505 to 1760 were connected to this college. Additionally, there are records of a small bell, bronze incense censer, bronze altar lamp and bronze cup and altar ewer all found at different times. Even with all of this evidence, it is not absolutely certain that a priest lived at Danag'ombe. However, all these items seem to have been in one cache, making it reasonably certain that Catholic Mass was celebrated in these wilds of Zimbabwe long before colonisation.

Owing to a lack of dateable imports from after 1750, it is unclear if the site was occupied after that time. Despite the great quantity of Portuguese and other trade goods, there is no foreign influence on the architecture.

Before colonisation, Danag'ombe was an incredibly important religious site for the local population. Writing in 1899, James Bryce described the mood on his visit there in 1895, during Johnson and Neal's diggings:

> At present it is not only uninhabited, but regarded by the natives with fear. They believe it to be haunted by the ghosts of the departed, and are unwilling, except in the daytime and for wages paid by the Exploration Company, to touch or even to enter the ruins. They can hardly be persuaded even to relate such traditions as exist regarding the place... The natives come sometimes to make offerings to ancestral ghosts, especially when they ask for success in hunting; and if the hunt be successful, strips of meat are cut off and placed in cleft sticks for the benefit of the ghosts.

These respectful attitudes by the local peoples are in line with the religious significance of several other stone-built ruins across the region. Many sites have a similar importance today to nearby communities. It is a delicate and necessary matter to allow them access to perform essential rituals and observances within their traditional religious mores and heritage laws.

The small site museum has much of interest for the visitor, including many of the original artefacts found at the site as well as information on the surrounding area. It rarely has electricity so bring a flashlight to see most of the exhibits. Due to its expansive size and the complex structures which hint at its important and far-reaching place in the history of this area, Danag'ombe remains one of the best ruins to see in Zimbabwe.

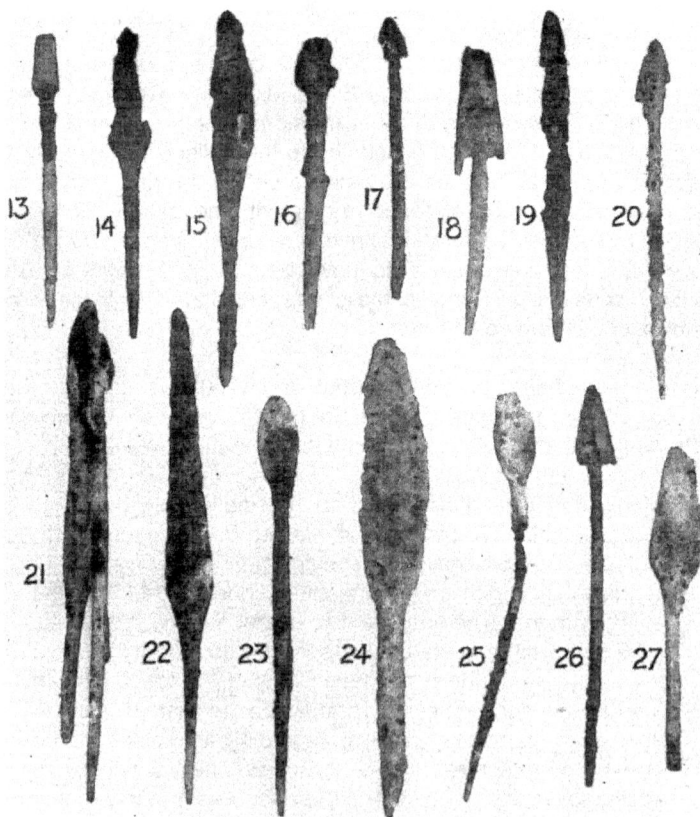

Some of the spears discovered during Randall-MacIver's excavations in 1905.

Naletale Heritage Site

This is easily the prettiest ruin in the country, made so by its fabulous setting, copious and intricate decoration and spectacular surrounding scenery. It is National Monument No. 3, declared so in 1937, immediately after Victoria Falls and Great Zimbabwe. Its beauty is enhanced by the lovely *Brachystegia* trees growing on the hill, as well as the many aloes (*A. chabaudii* and *A. excelsa*), rooting in the rocks.

The name Naletale is an Ndebele version of one of two possible Shona words, either of which may have been its original name. It was either *Nharetari* meaning "straight lines" referring to the wall decoration, or *Nhandare* that refers to the vast open grasslands one sees from the hilltop. The name was allegedly changed in the 1930s by a Native Commissioner who wanted it to be more Ndebele-like to reflect the incumbent residents.

Recent research shows that Naletale was built almost at the same time as Danag'ombe in the 17th Century. Owing to its pleasant location, with a near-constant breeze in the summer months, it is thought that it was built as a royal resort or, alternatively, an ancillary headquarters for the Torwa and Rozvi rulers. There are signs that a small population lived on the plateau on the hill slope below the main structures, perhaps working either as servants or custodians of the site when the rulers were not in residence. Early researchers mention evidence of gold working remains near the site, hinting at a possible function for control of production and trade of the precious mineral. Naletale was not in isolated splendour as there are several smaller sites in close proximity, including a small walled site on a kopje near the car park and ruins on surrounding hills, notably Gomoremhiko and Nharire Hill.

Naletale is a compact ruin and can be easily explored in a couple of hours. If possible, visit it in the late afternoon, to enjoy the best view of the granite walls turning golden in the glow of the sunset, the lovely landscape below bathed in luscious light.

The path to the summit is well-marked, several fading signs along the way explaining some of the history and conservation work done at the site. Sharp-eyed visitors will notice the change in the colour of the soil to an ashy grey about half-way up, the path being strewn with pottery shards and bone fragments. These are remnants of an old midden. Please do not remove anything from here or anywhere else at the site.

At this point, you will also notice two dolly holes located at what was once the edge of the village where the servants may have lived. Several people

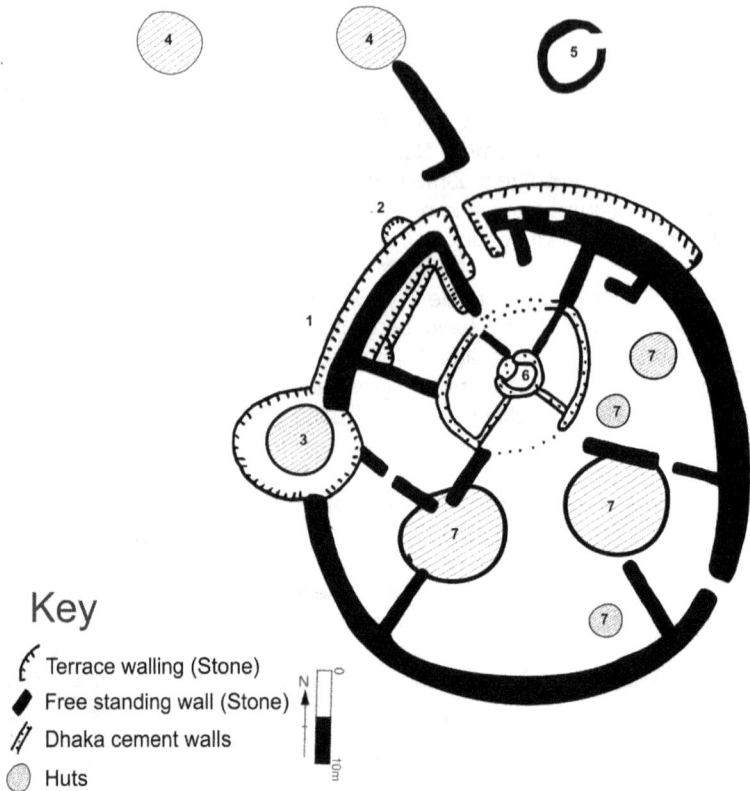

Key

𝄢 Terrace walling (Stone)
◗ Free standing wall (Stone)
🖋 Dhaka cement walls
◯ Huts

Map of the main area of Naletale

would have been needed to transport food and water the long distance up the hill to keep the elites happy and, in turn, to remove their rubbish and waste. There are the remains of several hut floors in this area, as well as foundations of grain bins, the food stores for the residents. The dolly holes were used for crushing and processing metal ore, possibly gold or iron. They are a common feature across Zimbabwe, and are different in shape and purpose from the grinding stones used for food processing in the past.

The first sighting of the front facade of Naletale (1) as you reach the summit is always a truly memorable moment. This profusely decorated wall combines almost every decorative style known from other Zimbabwe Culture sites. It is worth spending time drinking in the sight — at once unique and extraordinary.

The decoration is best observed on the massive front wall, although various elements may be observed on the outside of the entire enclosure. The small fragments of darker rock used in the banded and herringbone decoration is banded ironstone, brought here from 15 to 20 kilometres away where the main goldfields lie. The rest of the rock at the site is granite, quarried nearby.

There is a long, low clay-topped terrace at the base of the main wall, built into which is a low stone seat made of two steps (2), perhaps used by the king during audiences with his subjects.

The front facade of the main wall at Naletale

Naletale has the best decorated walling of any site in the country. As mentioned on page 11, much of the decoration is interpreted by some as a symbolic code, referring to the age, gender and status of the ruler and his immediate power structure. At Naletale in particular, the turrets can be seen as symbolic grain bins. Rozvi oral traditions hint at grain being left as offerings at these features, at this and other sites. In times past, it is suggested that each subsidiary chief would stand at their respective tower when presenting their tribute.

Protruding from the magnificent front wall is a large roughly-built stone platform (3), on top of which was built a large clay structure, perhaps a large hut for a senior court official such as a messenger or spirit medium. Unfortunately, the area was dug over by treasure hunters so it is difficult to deduce more. The platform was likely built after a collapse in the main wall, perhaps by the Rozvi people after they moved into the area. The hut was surrounded with several impressive elephant tusks, burned fragments of which were discovered during investigations in 1905.

Extending from the front of the main wall is a low, roughly-built stone wall, ending in the foundation of one of the stone platforms built on the top of the hill. Large houses were built on the outer platforms (4) which were presumably occupied by senior court officials.

To the north-east of the low wall is a small enclosure which was used as a cattle byre (5). Animals would have been kept here as symbols of wealth and also as sources of food for the elites who regularly ate beef. The main cattle byre is thought to be on a neighbouring hill, where a large flat area has been cleared and is covered with ancient cattle dung.

Entering the ruin through the splendidly-restored main entrance, one climbs up a large mound, once a massive central hut (6). When the site was first visited in the 1890s, this main entrance was closed off with a pile of rubble, with two narrow gangways providing access. Standing there, you will notice

Naletale's front entrance photographed in 1905 by David Randall-MacIver

there are seven stone walls radiating from the mound, their profiles broken by the foundations of large huts whose clay walls once merged with the stone ones. This creates an intricate network of enclosures with multiple purposes. Excavations done on the western edge of the central mound in 2018 showed three main phases of occupation, from the middle of the 17th century to the middle of the 20th century.

Excavations on the top of the mound in 1905, revealed a massive hut, 21 metres in diameter, made of nearly solid clay walls, almost half a metre thick. There is a second, smaller hut in the centre. The floor plaster was nearly 50cm thick. Radiating clay walls divided the space between the two huts into smaller compartments. The large hut would have been visible from outside the stone walls, clearly indicating the prestige of the ruler. The northern half of the building had no entrances from the rear, perhaps keeping that section solely for the ruler. It is here that the meat and beer for the personal consumption of the king may have been stored.

A stone-lined chamber was hidden beneath the floor of the inner hut, nearly two metres deep and about 1.2 metres at its widest. The top was only 38cm wide and was covered by a large stone, plastered with clay. It is likely that this chamber served as a latrine, collecting the waste produced by the ruler and his immediate family as a guard against potential witchcraft. Alternatively, it is possible that the chamber may have been used as a storage pit for spiritually valuable artefacts, but this is not certain.

There are five other houses, two enormous, in the main enclosure which were likely occupied by senior relatives of the king, possibly his wives. There are also several grain bin bases which stored the food for the ruler and his followers.

Some of the interior and exterior stone walls were covered with a clay plaster, often polished to a high sheen. When walking around the interior of the ruin, look carefully at different walls for faint traces of this plasterwork.

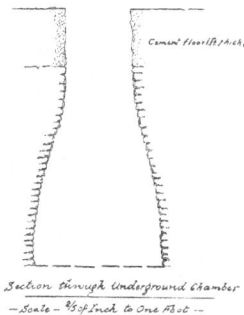

Randall-MacIver's sketch of the underground chamber, 1905

Not many finds are recorded from the archaeological investigations, while the treasure hunters left practically no records at all. Soapstone pipe bowls, used for smoking tobacco or *dagga* (marijuana), were found in the main enclosure, as were iron spear heads and tools, pottery fragments, copper wire and iron bracelets. A few glass beads and fragments of Chinese porcelain, dating to the late 17th and early 18th centuries, hint at wider trade connections. There are unreliable reports of gold crucibles and pellets being found somewhere at the ruins, evidence of smelting there, as well as gold beads, bangles, foil and small nails, the latter two possibly remnants of small wooden figurines once clothed in gold.

The site as we see it today is not in its original state. It has a long history of alterations to the stone walls. Treasure hunters destructively dug over the site before 1900. In 1904, J.L. Popham visited the site and published several valuable observations on its condition. In 1905, archaeologist David Randall-MacIver carried out excavations, the trenches from which are still visible in the hut platforms. D.M. Kirstein was made a curator of the site some time after 1905, removing several monoliths and, in 1937, reported that the front facade had deteriorated.

With Captain Stevenson, Kirstein used cement to hold together the top courses and restored the four monoliths visible today, but not in their original location. Today, use of a modern building material is not tolerated in restorations, but these men were guided by the use of clay plaster on a few walls at the site which they mistook for cement. In 1963, Roger Summers conducted excavations at the site and recovered ceramics with a few foreign imports, including glass beads and iron nails. In 1982, a collapse was recorded on the eastern side and restoration work was done by NMMZ and Chaplin High School students. Further problems were noted in the 1990s, with minor restoration and monitoring efforts being undertaken by the organisation.

In 2003 and 2004, a partial restoration of the eastern entrance and a section of walling on the southwestern side was undertaken by NMMZ. Between 2012 and 2014, with US$64,000 worth of funding from the U.S. Ambassador's Fund for Cultural Preservation, a team from NMMZ and various local universities restored much of the outer wall of the entire monument. A small site museum was completed at this time with brief displays on the history of the site and related structures. Surprisingly for only the third time in its history, further archaeological investigations were conducted in 2016, the results of which have informed this guide book.

Heading back down the hill and leaving this glorious site behind, the most exquisite landscape on every side, it's easy to imagine that this was once a place of peace, repose and happiness where the privileged came to enjoy the best of their kingdom and their reign. It's hard to visit and not feel that same sense of tranquility and joy.

The restored front entrance at Naletale

Naletale's eastern wall before restoration

Zinjanja Heritage Site

Although rarely visited owing to a lack of directional signage and a poorly-maintained access road, Zinjanja Ruins are one of the most fascinating in the Midlands. Their size and grandeur nearly match that of Danag'ombe (p.12) and, while barely studied, there is enough known to suggest tantalising possibilities about its role and function during the 17th and 18th centuries when it was built and occupied.

According to the *Matabele News and Mining Record* of Saturday, June 16, 1894, these ruins were initially named Regina, in honour of Queen Victoria as they were first visited on May 24, the Queen's birthday. The article describes the first known visit to the site by whites, including Dr Hans Sauer, friend of Rhodes and early land speculator in Bulawayo, Captain Wools Sampson and a Mr Bradley. Regrettably, these and other early visitors pillaged the ruin in their quest for gold, destroying much archaeological information in the process. Today the local name, Zinjanja, is preferred, perhaps referring to an extinct indigenous cattle breed — Njanja — although its exact meaning remains obscure. It is National Monument No. 102.

Dr. Hans Sauer describes his first visit in his book, *Ex Africa*:
> On examination, the temple proved to be a circular building in terraces diminishing in diameter upwards; there were three or four of these circular terraces, with steps leading from one to the other... They were quite flat and there were no outstanding features.

The site was probably built between 1649 and 1673, a time between the succession struggle and the Rozvi takeover by the Changamire. Zinjanja therefore post-dates Khami but was contemporary with Danag'ombe and Naletale. It was built either as a second potential capital site to replace Danag'ombe or, more likely, initially built and occupied by a rival claimant to the throne as a statement of their power. Zinjanja was very likely a competitor to Danag'ombe, but probably never surpassed it to become the regional capital.

Zinjanja consists of a central oval main platform (1) made up of multiple, stacked terraces, with a large enclosure (7) to the west. This was presumably a court suggested by the existence of a stone seat built into the densely decorated north wall overlooking the area, and several monoliths lining the northern section of the rough wall. As the ground slopes down

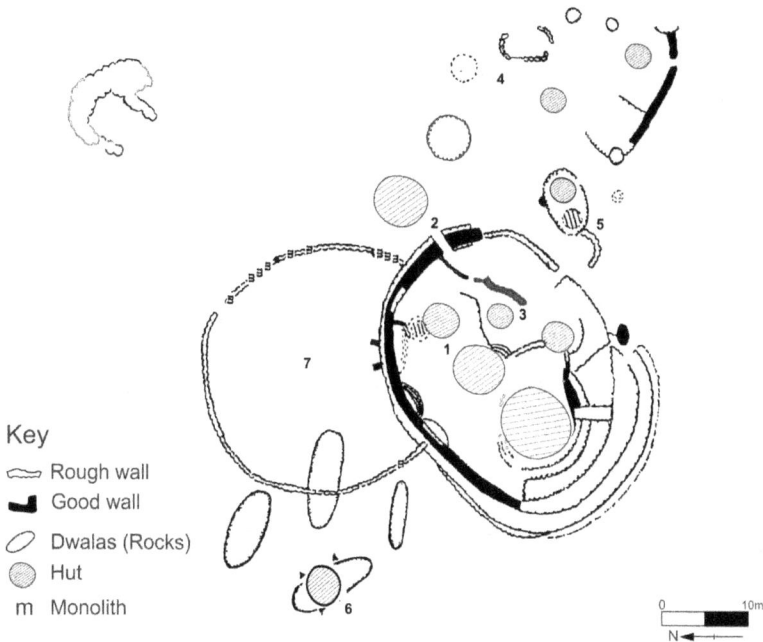

Key
- ⌒ Rough wall
- ◣ Good wall
- ⬭ Dwalas (Rocks)
- ◉ Hut
- m Monolith

Map of the central area of Zinjanja Heritage Site

toward the west and north-west, lower retaining walls of the main platform become rough freestanding walls forming an ill-defined enclosure.

The main entrance (2) to the central platform is large, nearly two metres wide. There are three niches in each wall of the entrance way, in which early visitors found remains of hardwood posts, some still standing with a fork at the top. These presumably carried strong cross beams with a small wall built on top of them, forming a formidable entry to the ruler's space, similar to those seen at Great Zimbabwe. One of the posts was removed and exhibited at a meeting of the Rhodesia Scientific Association in 1903, and a flat section was later sent to the South African Museum, Cape Town. This was analysed in 1976, with the outer layers dated to AD 1690, and identified as *Combretum imberbe*, or leadwood, a very hard wood excellent for building.

There are a few hut floors (3) on the main platform, likely the residence and utility buildings for the ruler. In addition, there is a great deal of hut dhaka scattered on the surface.

Part of the main facade of the central platform at Zinjanja

On his 1894 visit, Sauer described finding several flat stones on top of the terraces, arranged in a regular fashion which, when turned over, revealed a narrow hole, wider at the bottom than at the surface. Thinking there might be treasure to be had, Bradley, whom Sauer describes as a "freebooter", hired several men from the surrounding villages to excavate a drive (in the mining sense) through one of the terraces into one of the underground chambers. To their chagrin, they found it completely empty. Stating that he regretted this act of vandalism, Sauer went on to say, "The intriguing puzzle of the holes remained quite unsolved, the only possible explanation being that they had some religious significance".

There are at least eight of these chambers built into the main platform at Zinjanja, some of which have their bottom carved into the granite bedrock. Their function is not certain but an educated hypothesis may be made. As at Naletale (p.21), these chambers were possibly latrines collecting the waste of the ruler to prevent it being taken and used for malicious witchcraft. The number of chambers is excessive for that function alone and, alternatively, some may have functioned as temporary grain storages or even as emergency drains during heavy rain storms. More recent scientific excavations have not found any precise evidence as to their use, as most are lacking any sort of cultural materials to aid with interpretation.

Immediately north-east of the main area are numerous platforms (4) which, recent research has revealed, extend northward into an adjacent mountain and along its western slopes for almost a kilometre. Huts were built on these platforms and probably housed, among others, royal wives and senior court officials.

Entrance to one of the stone-lined chambers

The walling on the lower terrace of the main platform is of good quality, decorated with bands of check, chevron, perforated herringbone and cord decorations. Upper levels are in rougher style, largely undecorated, but were once covered in clay plaster polished to a high sheen resembling copper. This was mentioned by Sauer in his description of the ruins in 1894. The upper terraces are smaller in surface area but rise to at least six metres in height. Much of the walling on the south and southwest sections of the main platform has collapsed and is partly surrounded by rough walling, probably built as retaining walls.

A hut platform in front of the main entrance may have been the home of the equivalent of the king's seneschal. This man, in charge of the royal court, controlled access to the king and wielded immense personal political power in the court. There are several grain bin foundations on or near the main platform, as well as scattered among the platforms to the north. These were clearly domestic areas, the food stored used for cooking and brewing beer.

About 100 metres to the north-east is a formidable structure (5), massively built of rocks roughly piled to a height of at least three metres. It covers nearly 100 square metres. Its function is not entirely clear, although it may have been used by a senior male official involved with the administration of the women's area, as Tom Huffman has imaginatively argued. Alternatively, it may have been a later addition by a Rozvi ruler for a unique need, away from the Torwa constructions.

An unusual feature at Zinjanja is a small field of squat stone monoliths, partially buried in the ground, all nearly the same height. There are a few flat

The field of monoliths, likely the base for a grain bin

stones balancing on top of some of them, while the rest stand proud. Overly-imaginative early observers speculated about phallic worship and sex cults, but it is far more likely that these stones were once all covered with flat stones and a large grain bin, clearly visible to the surrounding population, built on top. There is a great deal of dhaka lying about in the immediate area which may well have come from this sort of structure.

Minor excavations were done in the 1990s by a team from NMMZ, aiming to investigate certain *dhaka* features to the north of the main platform. Excavations in 2016, recovered several glass beads, which analysis revealed had come from Europe, via the Indo-Pacific trade network. The beads from Zinjanja were made in the 17th to 18th Centuries.

The many large *Euphorbia ingens* growing from the collapsed walls add a great deal to the charm of this intriguing site, finally beginning to take its much-deserved place in the pantheon of magnificent sites bequeathed to us by the Torwa and Rozvi peoples from the mists of time.

Bhila Heritage Site

An elliptical ruin with a single entrance facing west, Bhila consists of a single, small enclosure, roughly 40 metres wide. A low platform flanks the northern side of the entrance. Closer inspection reveals that, at one point in history, the top of the platform was roughly paved with flat stones.

The walls are low, in places only a metre high, but very thick. The walling is crudely done, but there is some good quality walling near the entrance on the western side. What sets this site apart from similar ruins in the area is the large cairn field located to the north of the enclosure. More than 100 small piles of stone are located on the open edge of the dwala, forming a

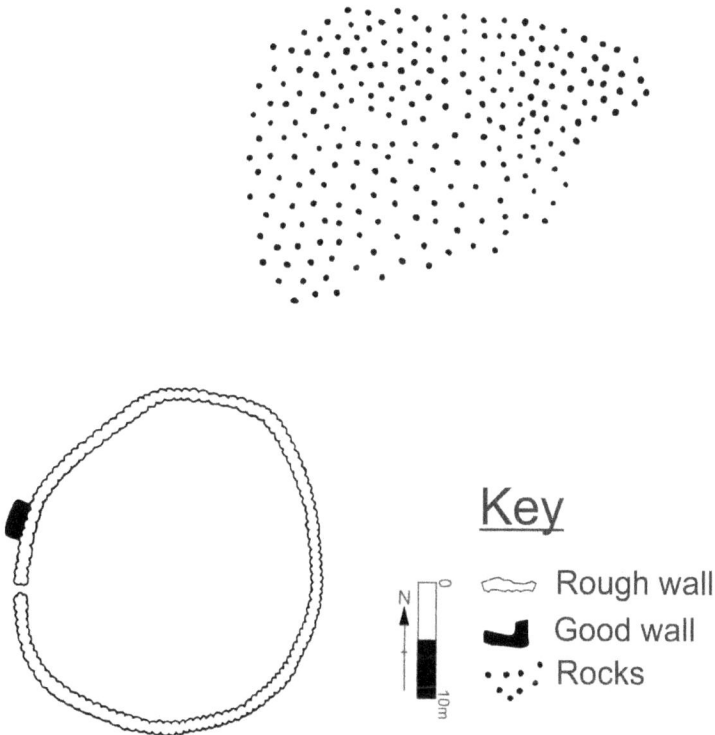

Key

〜	Rough wall
◣	Good wall
∴	Rocks

Map of the enclosure and neighbouring cairn field at Bhila

Roughly-built stone walling at Bhila

dense accumulation whose meaning and significance remains unclear. The ruin is heavily overgrown. The walls are being extensively damaged by the action of tree roots, and transient elephants walking over portions of the site. The soil within the enclosure is unusually barren and no pottery or other finds have been discovered on the surface; no professional excavations have been done at the time of writing. Warthogs, antelopes and bushpigs root about the site disturbing what deposit may exist. In Bhila's case, the lack of deposit, especially house remains, suggests a different function for the site.

Archaeologist, Tom Huffman, has argued Bhila served as a ritual site for the ruling elite of Torwa-Rozvi society. In a claim disputed by most other researchers, Huffman interprets the enclosure and associated cairns as the remains of an initiation centre for males — namely a circumcision lodge. The purpose of initiation lodges was to teach youngsters the rights and responsibilities of adulthood. The initiates had to be sequestered away from the rest of the population until they had completed their lessons and could be reintegrated into society. Various cultures in southern Africa, most notably the Venda and Sotho-Tswana, created initiation schools for males and females; the layout of the schools was different based on the needs of the sexes.

The cairns resemble graves, but Huffman argues these are symbolic resting places. At the end of Sotho-Tswana initiation schools, the initiates destroy all paraphernalia associated with childhood, burning their aprons, figurines and the like. The previous school's initiates then erect a cairn to symbolise the birth of the new age-set and regiment. "As a reversal, the cairns resemble graves, but symbolise rebirth". The fact that there are so many cairns at Bhila, especially when compared to similar sites in the region, suggests that it was in use for a considerable period of time. Alternatively, it can be argued that the site hosted several groups in a very short period of time.

Huffman's ideas about circumcision schools have been hotly contested. Some archaeologists accept the physical evidence but refuse to accept that the Shona were responsible, preferring later migrants such as the Sotho-Tswana. Indeed, the warlike Sotho, who passed through this area in the early 1830s during the second wave of the mfecane, are partly responsible for the collapse of the Rozvi state and may have built the structures theorised to be circumcision houses. Historians note the lack of reference in Portuguese documents and the absence of any oral traditions about initiation schools. There is currently no ethnographic, anthropological or other evidence for any of the Shona peoples practicing circumcision rituals in the pre-colonial past.

Part of the cairn field

There is a slight possibility that the BaLemba, a people with a Muslim-Jewish background, might have been responsible for creating and maintaining circumcision lodges in the south east of the country. Early travellers met these people in the interior of Zimbabwe and a few briefly mention such rituals. Huffman allows for the faint possibility (in his opinion) that Muslim traders could have been the sole practitioners for circumcision rituals on the Zimbabwean plateau.

More prosaically, the piles of stones to the north of Bhila ruin could simply be the quarried rock, waiting to be built into the existing wall, or to be used to create a new nearby enclosure. Until careful excavations are done, Bhila will remain an academic curiosity.

Whatever the significance of the site, the atmosphere is quite different to other ruins, perhaps due to its setting under the shade of trees which renders it dark, damp and somewhat eerie. The view from the cairn field on its rocky outcrop is quite magnificent and stretches as far as the eye can see. If you look carefully, you may be able to make out the walls of Naletale, some 11km away to the north-east.

Conservation Work at Stone-Walled Sites

Throughout this booklet you will have noted reference to the rebuilding of stone walls, clearing of deposit and other conservation strategies. Over the years Danag'ombe and Naletale have been subjected to considerable restoration and reconstruction. As discussed in the main text this has, in some instances, altered the very fabric of the site so attempts at explaining the traditional use of space and its changes over time have to be treated with caution. More recent work has been limited to repairing collapsing walls and repairing earlier reconstructions thought to be incorrect.

The National Museums & Monuments of Zimbabwe are in charge of all such conservation and recording programmes. The work follows strict guidelines in accordance with accepted international heritage ethics and procedures. The primary concern is to maintain authenticity, as defined in the UNESCO World Heritage Operational Guidelines, which relate to the "originality" of a monument and its essential values, however defined.

These ideals are not without their difficulties when put into practice. Even as the work done may meet all internationally-accepted guidelines, it is often the case that local people may bemoan the loss of the spiritual and sacred values caused by restoration work, research or tourism. Some even describe the monument as soulless, or feel the ancestors have been removed. There is a need to include local communities in such works to learn about their feelings and attitudes to such work, and respectfully and meaningfully integrate them with other priorities.

At many of the sites in the Insiza District, there is an ongoing structural monitoring programme, with visiting curators carefully checking the walls and watching for signs of imminent collapse. When necessary, and funds permitting, walls are dismantled, their foundations stabilised and then they are rebuilt as authentically as possible. During a visit to any of the sites covered in the book, you might see the museum's employees going about their work. Please feel free to ask them questions about their essential efforts in preserving some of Zimbabwe's most iconic archaeological sites.

Getting There

Please note that the sites discussed in this booklet fall under the auspices of the National Museums & Monuments of Zimbabwe. A custodian should be present at each of the sites and an entry fee is payable at Danag'ome and Naletale. The sites are reachable in a day trip from Bulawayo or Gweru.

Danag'ombe (Dhlo Dhlo, Danamombe)

These are reached by turning south off the Gweru-Bulawayo highway at Shangani. This dirt road crosses the railway; continue straight until reaching a T-junction after about 10km. There is a sign to the right, follow it for 12km. It can be rough in places. There is a signpost where you need to turn left, taking you along a short track to the site museum.

Naletale

If coming from Harare, turn off the main highway at Daisyfield (about 47km from Gweru). Ignore the Nalatale Siding road. Immediately turn left and then right across the railway line, then turn right again. After the junior school, turn left down a gravel road. Drive 23km on a decent dirt road, through beautiful farmlands. Just after a sharp turn to the right there is the house of the custodian at the right side of the road. Just beyond this is a track off to the right. Follow this to the car park and display.

If coming from Bulawayo, you can turn right at Shangani and follow the signs to Jabulani Safaris, passing via the new Shangani Sanctuary. You will find a signpost to Naletale after the first boom and you may follow the signposts from there.

Zinjanja (Regina)

Note: sign posting to Zinjanja Monument is practically non-existent, but local residents can guide visitors. Turn left at Insiza onto the dirt road heading south-east. After 45km you will reach Fort Rixon road junction; at 47km turn left towards Fort Rixon and travel through. After 55km turn right at the intersection, at 58km continue on at the road intersection, at 62km continue south at road intersection, at 66km turn left at road intersection.

Alternatively drive to Danan'ombe Monument, afterwards continue on the same dirt road, a further 11km to Fort Rixon, then south 24km to Zinjanja.

Bhila

Follow the signs to Jabulani Safaris. There used to be a signpost where to turn left to reach the monument. It is recommended to sign in at the office for Jabulani Safaris who will then provide precise directions to the monument.

Additional Reading

In addition to numerous articles published in academic journals, the following books, all with information on aspects of the Zimbabwe Culture, may be found in most good libraries:

Beach, D. 1994. *The Shona & their Neighbours*. Oxford: Blackwell.

Caton-Thompson, G. 1931. *The Zimbabwe culture: ruins and reactions*. Oxford: Clarendon Press.

Garlake, P. 1973. *Great Zimbabwe*. London: Thames and Hudson.

Hall, R. & Neal, W. 1904. *The Ancient Ruins of Rhodesia (2nd Edition)*. London: Methuen & Co.

Huffman, T. 1996. *Snakes & Crocodiles: power and symbolism in ancient Zimbabwe*. Johannesburg: Witwatersrand University Press.

Huffman, T. 2007. *Handbook to the Iron Age*. Scottsdale: University of KwaZulu-Natal Press.

Machiridza, L. 2018. *Archaeology of the Rozvi: Toward an Historical Archaeology of South-Western Zimbabwe*. Unpublished PhD Thesis, University of Pretoria.

Main, M. & Huffman, T. 2021. *Palaces of Stone: Uncovering Ancient Southern African Kingdoms*. Cape Town: Struik Travel & Heritage.

Manyanga, M. & Katsamudanga, S. (eds). 2013. *Zimbabwean Archaeology in the Post-Independence Era*. Harare: SAPES Books.

Mitchell, P. 2002. *The Archaeology of Southern Africa*. Cambridge: Cambridge University Press.

Pikirayi, I. 2001. *The Zimbabwe Culture*. Walnut Creek: Altamira Press.

Randall-MacIver, D. 1906. *Medieval Rhodesia*. London: Macmillan.

Sauer, H. 1973. *Ex Africa*. (Reprint). Bulawayo: Books of Rhodesia.

Summers, R. 1971. *Ancient ruins and vanished civilisations of southern Africa*. Cape Town: Bulpin.

van Waarden, C. 2012. *Butua and the End of an Era*. Cambridge: Cambridge Monographs in African Archaeology 82.

Banded Decoration

www.ingramcontent.com/pod-product-compliance
Lightning Source LLC
Chambersburg PA
CBHW071352280326
41927CB00041B/3055